"UM-SHMUM"

HOW THE UN AND ITS INSTITUTIONS BETRAY THE TRUST IN THEM

WHILE DEALING OBSESSIVELY WITH ISRAEL

Credit for the Map of Israel– © joeiera
Depositpohtos.com

Tel: +97254-8030648

Email: kobimnsil@gmail.com

Web site: www.kobisha.com

CLARIFICATION

As of early 2016, the world is in a general chaos. False hopes of many politicians and statesmen at the start of the new millennium of ending the era of wars were crushed to dust in the first decade of the millennium. The world today is much more dangerous. The widespread belief that the origin of the conflict in the Middle East is Israel`s refusal to make any progress in the negotiations with the Palestinians was shattered and has evaporated into thin air. Hundreds of conflicts and wars occur on the planet. Millions of refugees are flowing toward the Western countries and threaten to change their character forever. Syria and Iraq, that have ceased to exist long ago, are entangled in an all-out war with cross- interests in which the Americans, the Russians, the Saudis, the Iranians, the Turkish and God knows who else are involved. ISIS is progressing slowly toward its vision to impose Islam with the Sharia laws.

The UN, that was founded on the ruins of World War II in order to prevent the recurrence of such events, fails in its duty time after time. But there is one arena where the UN and its institutions reap fruits in abundance and that is the State of Israel. The focus and the many resources directed against Israel are enormous by any standard and they put in the shadow other crisis. The State of Israel is denounced and condemned time after time. The Human Rights Organization does not spare its rod against the only democracy in the Middle East. The indictments filed against Israel do not leave a shadow of a doubt – the State of Israel is a terror state, it tramples human rights, it commits war crimes and it should be denounced from every possible platform.

Is that so? Join me on a journey to discover the simple truth.

About the author

Kobi Shashoua is an author and a lecturer. Among his books you can find the most comprehensive book that exists to date bout the Israeli-Palestinian conflict "Israel: the truth, the whole truth and nothing but the truth." This book leads the reader chapter by chapter through the complex reality of the conflict and dissects the causes for the crisis, uncovers to the reader the true faces of the parties involved, and presents the tactics, the strategies and the true objectives, that lie below the surface. The author also wrote the book series: "Understanding the Middle East".The book you are holding in your hands is from that series.

The author, who resides in Israel, which is located in the most dangerous neighborhood of the world, in the heart of the Middle East, shares with us the facts together with the insights and the unique understanding of the region where he lives. We invite you to take part in this journey from a safe distance.

TABLE OF CONTENTS

FOREWORD

Imagine that you have registered to a new school. There are 204 students in that school. 57 of the students hate you. 100 of them are indifferent. You have few friends if any at all. During each break they are trying to hurt you, they tell lies and stories about you. Even those who are not really your friends begin to think that maybe it is better not to be your friend. Let's remember that there are still 100 students who do not understand what it is all about, but since 57 students slander you incessantly, the other 100 students as well can`t really stand you. It is not quite clear to them why, but they reckon that if 57 students hate you, there must be a good reason for that and that you for sure are to blame.

This is the situation in the UN today: out of 204 Member States in the UN [1], 57 are Muslim countries, 100 are non-aligned countries [2] and very few support Israel. So in this situation, there is no wonder that the UN neglects the business for which it was founded [3], and huge budgets stream to it but instead of trying to improve the situation on the planet by using them, considerable parts of these budgets are used for endless debates on the subject of delegitimizing the State of Israel.

For example: The UN Human Rights Council condemned Israel 4 times more than Syria, the second country in the order of countries condemned by the same Council [4]

MAKES NO SENSE!

---

[1] As of 2016.
[2] Countries that do not consider themselves aligned with any power bloc.
[3] Further on I shall expand about the purposes of the organization.
[4] http://eyeontheun.org.

The graph below shows the amount of condemnations directed at the State of Israel until 2010. Please note that the list does not include Syria yet because the graph was assembled before the outbreak of "The Arab Spring".

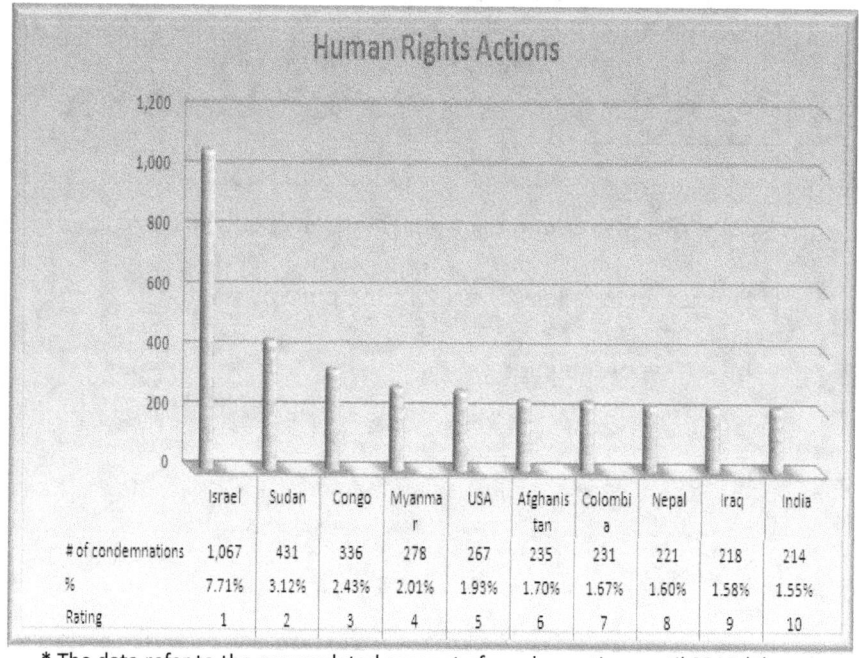

	Israel	Sudan	Congo	Myanmar	USA	Afghanistan	Colombia	Nepal	Iraq	India
# of condemnations	1,067	431	336	278	267	235	231	221	218	214
%	7.71%	3.12%	2.43%	2.01%	1.93%	1.70%	1.67%	1.60%	1.58%	1.55%
Rating	1	2	3	4	5	6	7	8	9	10

Human Rights Actions

* The data refer to the accumulated amount of condemnations until 2010 (5)

Suppose you say: what do you want, Israel is an occupier, a tormentor, the Heads of its army and government specialize in killing babies – a rhetoric designated to touch the soft belly of people since there is nothing worse than baby killers – after all it is written in many newspapers and is circulating on the Internet. Suppose for a minute that this is true, although in a democracy these things cannot happen on such large scales that they overshadow the state of emergency in Syria. Still, how is it possible that the State of Israel, with its territory that is just over a thousandth of the territory of the Middle East and has about 8 million residents has been condemned more than Iran, North Korea, Syria, Africa and other countries with such a significant gap? Does it seem logical to you?

MAKES NO SENSE!

(5) The data are from the website: Eyeon theun.

Genocide, known as the Darfur Massacre, was committed in Sudan during which 450,000 people were slaughtered and about 3,000,000 people were displaced from their villages. Much blood has been shed in Syria and in Iraq without having made any real attempts to stop it and the region seems to have turned into a wrestling arena between the Powers and between the Muslim factions among themselves. By the way, purge and obliteration of Christianity were performed in these regions. Hundreds of thousands of Christians were compelled to escape and to find themselves as refugees and those who stayed were massacred. The only country in the Middle East where the Christians are thriving and their population has grown is the State of Israel, the only democracy in the Middle East that is constantly condemned by the UN led by its Human Rights Council.

So what are actually Israel's "crimes" that justify such harsh condemnation?

Do you think that Israel really deserves such a considerable amount of condemnations?

It may well be that the brainwashing, financed by oil money, that you have been going through for years makes you think so, but take into account that the Muslim countries, about 57 countries, together with about another 100 non-aligned countries, constitute an automatic majority, that can initiate debates and endorse any resolution whatsoever. The only reason why no practical steps are taken against the "Zionist Entity" is that the United States exercises its right of veto time after time, and frustrates operational decisions to "punish" the only democracy in the Middle East!

UM-SHMUM

Um-Shmum is an expression coined by David Ben-Gurion [6] during a debate in a   government session on March 29th, 1955 to indicate the irrelevance of the UN when it comes to what is happening in the State of Israel.

---

[6] David Ben-Gurion was a leader in the struggle for the establishment of a Jewish state in Eretz Israel. He announced the establishment of the State of Israel (May 14th, 1948) and was its first Prime Minister.

The expression was stated after Moshe Sharett [7] responded to Ben-Gurion who said that it was necessary to expel the Egyptians from the Gaza Strip following the actions of the Fedayeen. [8] Moshe Sharett said that the UN will not accept such a move, and that it was necessary to treat the UN with respect, since had it not been for the UN the State of Israel would not have been established. Ben-Gurion elaborated and said: "It was only the audacity of the Jews that established the State, and not the decision of the U(N)M -

SHMUM". [9] An approximate translation of the expression would mean something like: **U**nited **N**othing.

I am sure that while reading these lines, many good people are outraged by such an expression for an organization that was founded in order to deal with the prevention of wars and crimes against humanity. But the UN does not fulfill its obligations and its objectives.

---

[7] The first Foreign Minister of the State of Israel.

[8] Fedayeen is a common name for various groups of infiltrators or of Palestinian terrorists, that operated in Israel during the fifties and the sixties.   From Wikipedia under the entry: "Fedayeen"

[9] From Wikipedia under the entry: "UM-SHMUM".

Let us briefly understand the background and the objectives that led to the establishment of the UN: at the end of World War II, in April-July 1945, an international conference was held in San-Francisco with the participation of representatives from 50 countries. In the conference it was decided to establish the United Nations Organization. The representatives in the conference have considered the matter of establishing the organization and endeavored to learn from past experience, so that the difficulties of "the League of Nations" [10] will   not be repeated.

[10] The League of Nations was an international organization founded on January 10th 1920, after World War I, by a decision of the Peace Conference in Paris, initiated by the President of the United States, Woodrow Wilson. The objectives of the League included the prevention of war by means of collective security, disarmament, settling disputes between countries through negotiations and diplomacy and the improvement of global welfare. According to the new world view, the organization was supposed to be the government of the governments with a defined role of settling disputes in an open forum that operates according to legal rules. Unlike a government institution, the League of Nations was established with no military or police force of its own, and was in fact dependent on the good will of the Member Powers to impose its decisions with their forces, which happened only rarely. Thus, during the thirties, the League of Nations was unable to prevent aggression by the fascist states, and the world slipped into the war that the organization was designed to prevent – World War II. The horrors of that war and the desire to prevent their recurrence were the basis for the establishment of the international organization that replaced the League of Nations, the United Nations. But similar to its predecessor, the United Nations as well failed to evolve into a world government institution, and it, as well, is inflicted with weaknesses that prevent him from fulfilling its purposes. From Wikipedia under the entry: "League of Nations".

At the end of the discussions, on June 26th, the Charter of the United Nations was signed. The Charter opens with a solemn declaration about the goals and the principles of the organization: the peoples of the United Nations are partners in whatever possible to prevent future wars, to reaffirm faith in fundamental human rights, to maintain justice and to promote social progress.

Moreover, the UN was established: to treat one another with tolerance and with confidence and live together in peace, and to join forces to accomplish these two things, and to ensure the non-use of armed forces. [11]

Purposes:

- ✓ To ensure the maintenance of international peace and security and to take joint actions in order to eliminate factors that threaten these goals, and to prevent international disputes (as aforesaid: a stunning success, since currently there are only about 424 disputes around the world). [12]
- ✓ To endeavor to foster friendly relations between nations, while maintaining mutual respect and the right to self-determination of nations (as aforesaid: a huge success in the Middle East!)

- ✓ To reach international co-operation on the subjects of: economy, society, culture, respect of human rights etc. (as aforesaid: a huge success. Trade war between the United States and China, revival of the Cold War between Russia and the United States, a clash of the Islam and the West, "respect" of human rights in Africa, Iran, Syria, Iraq, North Korea and my apologies to the countries I omitted).
- ✓ To be a centre for consolidating the activities of the nations (I know it sounds cynical and spiteful, but it seems that the UN is united mainly about anti-Israel resolutions). One of the nicknames I was exposed to was UNAI namely **U**nited **N**ations **a**gainst **I**srael.

---

(11) From Wikipedia under the entry: "United Nations".

(12) The data was taken from the Conflict Barometer 2014 report by the Heidelberg Institute For International Conflict Research e.V

There is no doubt that calling such a respectable institution "UM-SHMUM" is an insult and humiliation. These are meanness and nastiness of the "Zionist conquerors" that prove their conceit and arrogance.

But let me offer you a slightly different perspective (a tasting of which you have already received regarding the main work of the UN Human Rights Council) and judge for yourself.

Accepting things at face value is a convenient way to divert public opinion through continuous publication of false assumptions and facts.

Is it really about the United Nations of which we can all be proud and pronounce its name with pride, or is it about some kind of an attempt to unify which is cynically exploited by global power-blocs that use its resources, its prestige, its name and its institutions in order to promote only their narrow interests – and damn the world!

The only thing that is decided in the UN is not to decide, unless the decisions are against Israel. Many people are unaware of what is going on and I would like to enlighten you. Join me for an open minded journey about the UN, its work, its achievements and its modus operandi. Fasten your seat belts and tilt the back of your seat because we are entering a storm.

THE AUTOMATIC MAJORITY

The automatic majority: In the UN there is an automatic majority of 57 Muslim countries and 100 non-aligned countries that are able, in principle, to pass any resolution they want against Israel. And so they do. Countries that are in a state of internal wars, countries that human rights is a foreign concept to them, dictatorships that commit massacres and genocide, all these vote again and again against the only democracy in the Middle East, that is struggling to defend itself while adopting moral values that are unmatched in the world.

The organization is headed by the Secretary General of the UN who is appointed for a period of 5 years. Among the past Secretary Generals, were some that it is doubtful whether their opinions and activities were consistent with the goals of the UN as mentioned above. On January 1st, 1972 Kurt Waldheim was appointed Secretary General of the UN for 2 consecutive terms of office. In 1986 he was running for President of Austria. During his candidacy for the position it was revealed that during World War II, Kurt Waldheim served as an officer in the Wehrmacht [13] that committed war crimes. This fact led to boycott of Waldheim by the Western leaders.

In 1975, during his term of office, a resolution was passed in the UN equating Zionism with racism. There is no point discussing the matter, let it only be noted that after 16 years the UN retracted its resolution and nullified it.

In 1976, in a blatant anti-Israel remark, Waldheim called "Operation Entebbe" that was aimed to rescue hostages, a "flagrant aggression". I think that "Operation Entebbe" is the most daring operation in the history of rescuing abductees. The operation proved Israel's obligation to its citizens. I don`t think that this operation can be duplicated, and I don`t think that there will be an operation that will overshadow with its splendor "Operation Entebbe".

Nevertheless, the UN Secretary General Kurt Waldheim saw fit, as the representative of the UN, to call it "a flagrant aggression". I will elaborate briefly about the operation. I assume you can feel, particularly in light of the remarkable success of Osama Bin Laden in toppling the Twin Towers, that aerial terror has become part of the arsenal of discussions of radical Islam. Well, aerial terror is an old invention that is rooted in the 60's of the last century.

---

(13) Wehrmacht was the official name of the army of Nazi Germany 1935-1945. During the years of its operation about 18 million soldiers served in the Wehrmacht. About 5 million of them were killed in battle – mainly during World War II, and about 11 million were captured. The Wehrmacht was one of those responsible for the Holocaust, and many of its senior officers were sentenced for their involvement in this crime and in other war crimes.

On the 27th of June 1976 an "Air France" aircraft was hijacked, after a stopover in Athens. [14] There were 248 passengers on the plane and 12 crew members. After a stopover in Benghazi, Libya, the plane took off to Entebbe, Uganda, about 3,800 kilometers away from Israel. The 2 German terrorists, members of the "Revolution Cells" and the 2 Palestinian terrorists, members of the "Popular Front for the Liberation of Palestine" were joined by 4 Palestinian terrorists.

On July 29th, the Israeli and the Jewish passengers were assembled in the passengers hall of the old terminal at the airport, and the rest of the passengers were released.

At that time, it was not customary to hijack aircrafts in order to smash them on buildings. The demands of the terrorist were more "modest" and amounted to the release of 40 terrorists imprisoned in Israel, five terrorists imprisoned in Kenya, six anarchists imprisoned in Germany, one anarchist imprisoned in Switzerland and another one in France. In addition, they demanded ransom. If their demands were not met by July 1st, all the hostages would be executed. Israel got an extension of the ultimatum until July 4th.

While conducting the negotiations the IDF [15] started to plan a rescue operation, based on the intelligence data about the Entebbe airport. On July 3rd 4 Hercules aircrafts of the Israeli air force took off from Sharm el-Sheikh and flew to Entebbe. When they were over Ethiopia they received the government approval to proceed with the operation.

The fighters arrived on time, and managed to land the aircrafts successfully although the landing lights at the airport went out. The rescue forces proceeded from the aircrafts toward the terminal in several jeeps, headed by a Mercedes which was the exact replica of Idi Amin`s, the President of Uganda, car. In the terminal building an exchange of fire began between the IDF soldiers and the terrorists.

---

[14] The description of "Operation Entebbe" is taken from Wikipedia under the entry: "Operation Thunderbolt".

[15] Israel Defense Forces.

The hostage Ida Borowitz was killed by the terrorists, and when the rescuers entered, a 19-year-old youngster named Jean Jacques Maimony got up, and the IDF soldiers shot him by accident.

The passengers were transferred to the Hercules aircrafts that flew to Kenya where they refueled and then continued on to Israel.

The codename given to the operation at the time of its preparations was "Operation Thunderbolt". After the operation it was given the name "Operation Jonathan" in honor of Lt. Col. Jonathan Netanyahu (the brother of the Israeli Prime Minister, Benjamin Netanyahu) who was killed during the operation. In Israel and in the world it is known as "Operation Entebbe". The fighters destroyed eight Mig aircrafts that were parked at the airport, in order to prevent pursuit after the air force planes.

Israel won acclaim in the Western world following the bold operation. France expressed its satisfaction for the rescue of the hostages; Germany referred to the operation as "an emergency operation and self-defense", and Switzerland congratulated Israel.

Britain and the United States were particularly impressed by the operation and referred to it as "mission impossible"; In the United States they even saw some symbolism in the date the hostages were released – the fourth of July, celebrating that year the Bicentennial Independence Day of the United States.

The hostage-rescue mission is supposed to be an operation that makes every free citizen proud, but the Communist bloc and the Arab world condemned the operation.

Egypt, Syria, Iraq and Yemen, some of whom even denounced the kidnappers during the hijacking, denounced now the action of the IDF as forfeiting human lives and harming freedom fighters.

The Soviet Union accused Israel of incursion into a free peace loving country and undermining its sovereignty.

The UN condemned Israel, and its secretary, Kurt Waldheim, referred to the operation as "a flagrant aggression"!

If so, is it not justified to name it: "UM-SHMUM"?

MAKES NO SENSE!

THE UN AND ISRAEL

At the beginning of the chapter it was specified that one of the goals of the UN is to endeavor to foster friendly relations among the various peoples, while maintaining mutual respect and the right to self-determination of states <u>except for the State of Israel</u>:

Israel is not a full participant in the committees of the UN. [16]

Most of the UN activity, that includes elections to UN bodies, negotiations behind closed doors, and sharing information, is conducted in the context of 5 regional groups: Africa, Asia, Eastern Europe, Latin America and the Caribbean islands, Western Europe and other groups (WEOG). [17]

Some of the WEOG countries refuse to accept the State of Israel as a full-fledged member, while hiding behind the European Union`s facade. These countries include France, Greece, Ireland, Netherland, New-Zealand, Portugal, Switzerland and Britain.

Denying full-fledged membership constitutes a blatant violation of the United Nations Charter that pledges "equal rights of nations large and small".

Um-Shmum.

---

(6) From the website Eyeontheun.

(17) Western European and Other Groups

Ahmadinejad at UN General Assembly AFP
PHOTO / TIMOTHY A. CLARY

Leaders from around the world come to the UN, unfold their political doctrine and offer suggestions on how to promote the sublime goals of the UN. A typical example is the speech given by the President of Iran (who led, during his tenure, the issue of Holocaust denial in the world) at the UN General Assembly on the 23/09/2008. The essence of the speech: at the outset the speech deals with the principles of equality, justice, acceptance and thanksgiving to Allah for all the good things.

Afterwards, the President of Iran spoke about the ailments of the world and about those responsible for them, "the criminal Zionist conquerors", who have been killing Palestinians for over 60 years. [18]

According to him, the Zionists gathered people from all over the world and brought them to a country that belongs to other people, whom they murder.

He said that due to the support of the Powers in the "Zionist murderers", the Security Council is paralyzed. In addition, he made sure to mention the "Protocols of the Elders of Zion" when he attacked the handful of Zionist liars who play around with the decency, the integrity and the rights of the European and the American nations.

Even though the Zionists are a tiny minority, they control the economic centers and the political junctions in the European and the American states.

---

(18) The content of the speech is from the article: "The President of Iran at the United Nations: Zionist thugs control the world" by Dana Zimmerman, 24.09.08. From the YNET website.

During elections, candidates visit the Zionists in the conferences they hold, and pledge to support their interests in order to get their votes...Thus these nations are wasting valuable resources on the crimes and the conquests of the Zionists contrary to the interest of these nations.

The Zionists think that they are superior to others.....they continue with their cruelty and their domination, and are therefore the root of the problems in human society nowadays.

According to him, his country is developing nuclear reactors for peaceful purposes.

Apart from rearming, developing and producing missiles, enriching uranium, inaugurating nuclear facilities, supporting the Hezbollah and the Hamas, training suicide bombers, threatening to destroy Israel, Iran has no political and nationalistic aspirations or nuclear and military programs.

This reminds me of science fiction movies where hostile aliens declare: "We come in peace".

At the end of his speech, the Iranian President received a standing ovation from the delegates who attended his lecture at the UN.

MAKES NO SENSE!

Um-Shmum – did we say already?

The UN was established in order to prevent the recurrence of the atrocities and the genocide that happened during World War II. It seems that the mere fact of delivering such a hateful speech that is applauded in the UN, indicates that the UN institutions betray blatantly the founders of the organization.

You don`t believe? Well, let us check what happened in Rwanda with the knowledge of the UN.[19]

(19) The following paragraphs were taken from Wikipedia under the entry: "Genocide in Rwanda".

In 1994 genocide occurred in Rwanda, during which mass murder of thousands of citizens of the Tutsi clan, as well as moderates of the Hutu clan was committed during a civil war. The genocide lasted for about 100 days, from the 6th of April until mid-July 1994. The number of victims was about 800,000 of the Tutsi clan and hundreds moderates of the Hutu clan. Other estimates quote much higher numbers, up to 1,000,000!

Preparations for the genocide were made already at the beginning of 1994. These did not go unnoticed by the UN. In January 1994 the Commander of UN forces in Rwanda received information according to which the Hutus have started their preparations to murder the Tutsis. He passed on this information to the Military Adviser of the UN Secretary General. The UN rejected the request of the Commander of the forces to intervene, because it exceeded the mandate set to the UN forces. Instead the UN settled for a warning to the President of Rwanda!

MAKES NO SENSE!

The militiamen murdered their victims mostly with machete knives. Soldiers used also firearms. Local leaders called on the citizens to murder their neighbors the Tutsis. Those who refused to participate were sometimes killed themselves. Catholic priests and citizens tried to hide people from the killers, but in many cases the priests were unable to rescue, and some even took active part in the murder. In one case, more than 5,000 people, mostly Tutsis, found refuge in a chu Shutterstock/robtek the town of Ntaramn. The militiamen fired into the church, threw in hand grenades, and killed all the people that were in the church, except for 25 survivors. In another case 1,500 Tutsis found refuge in a church in Kivomo. Local residents, who joined the militia, used bulldozers to demolish the building with its occupants. Anyone who tried to escape was slaughtered with machetes.

How did the UN react to the genocide that was committed with its knowledge? During most of that period the UN instructed the Commander of UN forces in Rwanda to focus on assisting in the evacuation of the foreign citizens from the country.

On the 29th of April 1994 the UN admitted that "it may be that acts of genocide have been committed in Rwanda". According to Red Cross estimates, about 500,000 Rwandans have already been killed until then. The UN agreed to send 5,500 soldiers to Rwanda, most of them from African countries. But the deployment of the troops was delayed because of disputes over their funding.

On June 22nd, the UN Security Council allowed France to land troops in the city of Goma in the territory of Zaire (today the Democratic Republic of Congo) for the purpose of humanitarian aid. The French troops deployed in south-west Rwanda and managed to stop the violence there, but in many cases the troops arrived only after the Tutsis have already been murdered or deported.

According to various estimates, within three and a half months between 800,000 and 1,000,000 people were killed in Rwanda.

Since the Rwanda genocide, countless atrocities have occurred. Some of them were so enormous that it was impossible to ignore them, for example the wars in Syria, Iraq, Yemen, Libya etc. Atrocities continue to happen in these moments all over the world, but for some reason, a conflict that in terms of its geographical size and the number of people involved in it was supposed to be marginalized is the only one that features permanently in the headlines.

The UN continues to discuss the violent crimes committed by the Zionist regime in the Gaza Strip (the facts are that until the start of operation Cast Lead [20] over 9,000 missiles were fired on Israeli cities) and to condemn Israel again and again.

The UN discusses over and over the problem of the Palestinian refugees, while tens of millions of refugees are stranded all over the world without holding even one discussion about them.

Did you know, for example, that at the beginning of the millennium there was another World War? Did you hear about it? Did the UN interfere – no. The UN has no time, it is busy condemning Israel. Did you hear about the Second Congo War? Do you even know that a country by that name exists? Maybe yes maybe no.

---

[20] Operation Cast Lead was a response to the constant firing of missiles from the Gaza Strip toward the southern cities of the State of Israel. The operation started on Saturday December 27th 2008 and ended on January 21st.

The Second Congo War [21] took place in the years 1998 - 2003, mainly in the Democratic Republic of Congo (formerly Zaire).

9 African countries and about 20 armed groups participated in this war that was called "The World War of Africa" or "The Great War of Africa".

The death toll following the war was about 5.4 million people, mostly from hunger and diseases. Millions more have been displaced or have found refuge in neighboring countries.

Despite its official end in 2003, violence continued in a large part of the eastern region of the country. The estimates in 2004 were that about 1,000 people were dying daily from violence, hunger and lack of medications. The continuation of the fighting led to forced emigration toward neighboring countries.

MAKES NO SENSE!

During the Darfur massacre as well, when about 450,000 people were slaughtered between the years 2003-2009, the UN did not taken an active stand but wasted time. Hundreds of thousands of victims were slaughtered, raped and robbed. The UN not only did not take a stand, it also took part in these crimes.

In an investigative report published in the British Daily Telegraph [22], allegations were made about rape of girls in Darfur by UN soldiers.

MAKES NO SENSE!

---

[21] From Wikipedia, under the entry: "Second Congo war".

[22] "UN staff accused of raping children in Sudan", Kate Holt and Sarah Hughes, 02.01.07.

THE ACTIVITIES OF THE UN

So what does the UN actually do?

Let's check:

The first Durban Conference [23]: Following resolution 52/111 passed by the UN in 1997, it was decided to convene in Durban in South Africa a conference to deal with racism and xenophobia. The conference was held in September 2001.

Preparations for the conference have been made a year earlier through 4 Regional Conferences: A conference for the European states, a conference for the states in the Americas, a conference for the states in Africa and a conference for the states in Asia. The Asian conference was held in Tehran with the participation of the Muslim States Organization, and Israel, of course, was not allowed to participate. In the Regional Conference in Tehran a severe indictment against Israel was filed by the Muslim states that included 7 paragraphs:

1. Israel is an apartheid state and should therefore be boycotted and the countries that support Israel should be condemned.
2. Israel is an occupying state. Occupation is a crime against humanity and endangers world

peace.

3. Zionism is racism.

4. Israel is violating the human rights of the Palestinians. 5. Israel is committing genocide, war crimes and crimes against humanity, and therefore an armed struggle should be conducted against it.

6. There isn't one Holocaust. There is no uniqueness in the Holocaust of the Jewish people against disasters suffered by other peoples in the world, such as the slavery of the black people in Africa or the "Holocaust" committed by Israel against the Palestinians.

7. The State of Israel exists in sin. It was established by an ethnic purge of the Arabs in its territory.

Thus, instead of channeling UN resources to find solutions or to take actions to global eradication of racism and xenophobia, there is an enormous waste of resources dictated by Muslim and Arab states whose purpose is to shift the attention toward delegitimizing Israel, the only democracy in the Middle East.

---

[23] Based on the entry: "United Nations Conference against Racism (2001)" from Wikipedia.

Outside the Convention Center, thousands of people from different organizations   march protesting mainly against the "crimes" committed by Israel (AFP Photo).

("Peace activists" in a support rally for the eradication of racism and xenophobia outside the Durban Conference 2001)

While the Durban Conference was discussing the violation of human rights in the State of Israel, Israel had to deal with daily terrorist attacks on its citizens by   suicide bombers who blew themselves up at bus stops, at coffee shops, in crowded places, in a hotel where the Seder was celebrated. The attacks claimed heavy casualties in the country, and as a result the State of Israel started to build a security fence as a barrier between the areas where the Palestinians live and the territory of Israel.

Three days after the Conference adjourned a terrorist attack hit the USA destroying the Twin Towers (11/09/2001). The spotlight moved immediately toward radical Islam.

When the Twin Tower attack happened many voices against Israel were heard. For instance: had the USA not supported Israel unreservedly, the attacks would not have hit its soil.

These are arguments of ignorance. The truth is that Israel is perceived by radical Islam as a branch of the United States in the Middle East. According to their perception, the State of Israel is the offshoot of American imperialism. From their point of view, let`s finish off with Israel first, and then move on to the United States.

Sounds illogical? Read what the President of Iran said on this matter in a seminar that was held on October 26th 2005 entitled: "A world without Zionists": "God willing, soon we will experience a world without the United States and without the Zionists." While the words of the Ayatollah Ruhollah Khomeini were echoing in the background, Ahmadinejad continued his speech, "As the Imam has said, Israel must be wiped off the map."

What motivates it? The President of Iran has the answer:

"Throughout history a war has been going on between the arrogant and   conceited world and the Muslim world. In this historic war, the battle fields have moved many times. Sometimes the Muslims had the upper hand. Unfortunately, in the last three hundred years, the Muslim world has retreated from the arrogant and conceited world. A hundred years ago the last bastion of Islam fell, when the attackers created the "Zionist entity". This entity is used as a front stronghold to propagate their goals in the heart of the Muslim world. The crucial fate on the historic war will be decided in Palestine. There are those who wonder if the day   will come when the world be without the United States and the Zionists....this goal is indeed achievable. There is no doubt that a new wave will wash away in Palestine the disgraceful blemish off the face of the Muslim world". (24

In 2009 another Conference against racism was held in Durban. This time the 10 Western countries, amongst them the United States,

Canada, Australia and Holland boycotted the Conference, for fear that most of the time will be dedicated to "The crimes of the State of Israel".

Unsurprisingly the Conference opened on "Holocaust day". The President of Iran, the pursuer of justice and peace, a Holocaust denier who has threatened several times to annihilate the State of Israel and who propagates his teachings through the financing of world terrorism, was invited to the Conference.

---

(24) From the website http://www.globalsecurity.org/military/world/iran/zionist-entity-2.htm.

As usual, the speech made by the President of Iran was full of hope for a better   and just future, and a world where it will be easier to live and if possible, without Israel.

He claimed repeatedly that Israel is committing genocide in the Gaza Strip, while ignoring the Iraq-Iran war (1980-1988) where over 1,000,000 people have been killed. But that was a war between Muslims and this, of course, is alright.

And millions of dead are not counted. Since then, of course, a few hundreds of thousands Muslims more have been added during "The Arab Spring".

MAKES NO SENSE!

THE INTERNATIONAL ATOMIC ENERGY AGENCY

The International Atomic Energy Agency: On July 29th 1957 the International Atomic Energy Agency was established. The initiative to establish the agency came from the UN and the USA. The purpose of the agency is to promote the use of atomic energy for civilian purposes, and to prevent its use for military purposes.

Muhammad El Baradei was the Director General of the Agency from December 1997 until November 2009. In recent years Iran has been developing nuclear technology. Nuclear reactors are being built throughout the country and a game of cat and mouse goes on with Iran. The Iranians continue to claim that they have the right to develop nuclear technology for peaceful purposes, while on the other hand the President of Iran has been emphasizing from every available platform his desire to destroy the "Zionist entity". This fact, of course, did not prevent the powers from signing on July 14th 2015 an agreement regarding the Iranian nuclear program so that it could stay on nuclear threshold and work even more so to achieve its aspirations.

The International Atomic Energy Agency continues to look for evidence that Iran is developing nuclear technology for military uses, evidence that every intelligence satellite and western intelligence agency have found already years ago. It is likely that the Ostrich Policy (that buries its head in the sand) will eventually cause a long-term damage, but who really cares?

On September 17th 2009, the American news agency AP published a confidential   report by the International Atomic Energy Agency, which claims that Iran has enough know-how to manufacture an atomic bomb. In addition it was claimed that Muhammad El-Baradei, the Head of the Atomic Energy Agency, concealed this information. El-Baradei denied these allegations and said that the motive for these accusations is political.

The International Atomic Energy Agency clarified that despite reports in the media, there is no proof that Iran has a military plan.

Thus Iran continues to work diligently to attain a nuclear bomb for "peaceful purposes", and the

Atomic Energy Agency continues to look for evidence.

Eventually, one fine day Iran will announce that it possesses a nuclear bomb, and the world will be flabbergasted and recriminations will go back and forth in the International Atomic Energy Agency.

On September 6th 2007 Israeli air force planes attacked buildings in Syria. About six months after the attack, US Government officials announced that the target that was attacked and destroyed was a nuclear reactor for the production plutonium still under construction, built in Syria with the assistance of North Korea. [25]

At the time Syria was a dictatorship that maintained extensive ties with Iran and North Korea, and if anyone believes that developing the reactor was for peaceful purposes, he is kindly invited for hospitalization. In fact, had it not been for the destruction of the reactor while still under construction the world would have had to face a much more serious danger. Just imagine how the world would have looked if ISIS had access to nuclear weapon.

---

[25] Israeli air force attack in Syria (2007), from Wikipedia.

In response to the bombing of the Syrian reactor, El-Baradei, Chairman of the International Atomic Energy Agency, blamed Israel for violating international law, saying that the Israeli attack prevented from the Agency the possibility to fulfill its duty to detect illegal nuclear activity.

In addition, he reminded that it was not the first time that Israel was violating blatantly international law by attacking a nuclear reactor (more on that later).

The mere attack of the reactor in Syria prevented the Agency from fulfilling its duty to detect illegal nuclear activity. It is impossible to deny the logic in this argument, since the International Atomic Energy Agency has already proved in the past its ability to detect illegal activity and to stop it. For example: the detection and the prevention of North Korea from being equipped with a nuclear bomb, a success the dimensions of which were revealed on October 9th 2006, when North Korea conducted its first nuclear test.

Needless to say that since then Korea has conducted 3 more nuclear tests, the latest one was with a hydrogen bomb on January 6th 2016.

This is not the first time that Israel "violates international law" and bombs a nuclear reactor prior to its completion. On July 7th 1981 Israel carried out an air raid on the Iraqi nuclear reactor that was towards becoming operational. Of course that was a flagrant violation of international law. A year earlier Saddam Hussein, the President of Iraq, made an aggressive speech and reiterated his desire to destroy the State of Israel. But the world, that has already proved throughout history how important it was to protect the Jews, did not think like the government of Israel. As expected, two weeks after the attack the UN General Assembly and the Security Council adopted a resolution strongly condemning Israel.

In the following decade, during the First Gulf war, Iraq launched scud missiles on Israel, although Israel did not take part in the war. Israel became unwillingly the scapegoat of the war. During the Gulf War 39 missiles were fired toward Tel-Aviv, Haifa and the Negev. The scud missiles caused extensive damage to property, many injuries and one killed. The American pressure prevented Israel from retaliating against the Iraqi aggression, and the policy of restraint adopted by the Israeli government led to sympathy and support in the wide world. The Palestinian population in Judea and Samaria and in the Gaza Strip, on the other hand, organized spontaneous support rallies in Saddam Hussein, and many have cheered from the rooftops while rockets were falling in population centers in the State of Israel.

When the First Gulf War erupted, I was an 18-year-old student in my last year of high school. In the months prior to operation "Desert Storm" [26], Saddam Hussein did not stop threatening that he would burn and destroy the entire State of Israel. The government of Israel started to distribute protection kits to the residents. The kits contained gas masks and syringes for the treatment of poisoning by nerve gas. Every resident in the State of Israel received such a kit, and had to carry it with him everywhere. In addition, we were asked to prepare in every apartment a sealed room by sealing door frames and to tighten glass panels by pasting masking tapes criss-cross.

In the sealed room we prepared emergency supplies including water, foodstuff, blankets, radios, flashlights, batteries etc. The country is tiny, so we could hear all the hits of the rockets that were fired on the Tel-Aviv area. The noise was terrifying, and from the moment the sirens

sounded until the hit a few minutes   passed
during which we prayed that the rocket will not
fall on us or near us. Sometimes, about a minute
before the hit we could hear the launching of the
Patriot missiles. [27] Once a missile fell about 300
meters from our house. Following the blast, the
glass panels in shops and in apartments in our
vicinity were shattered. The anxiety was
unbearable. The hospitals were filled with panic
stricken people. Many citizens injected
themselves atropine [28], convinced that nerve gas
has filtered into the sealed room and will soon
cause them to die in agony.

---

[26] The First Gulf War 02/08/90-28/02/91.

[27] Anti-aircraft missiles converted into anti-ballistic
missiles that were not too successful at the time...

[28] Medication that serves as a treatment for poisoning by
nerve gas.

The residents of the country carried their
protection kits on their shoulders every day, and
planned meticulously where they could find

shelter from the moment the sirens sounded until the hit of the rockets (after about 7 minutes on average). The trauma and the anxiety continued to haunt us long after the fighting ended. Each sound reminiscent of the siren, made the heart miss a beat and the body to shrink.

The most grateful for the bombing of the reactor were the Saudis, who have been attacked during operation "Desert Storm" by missiles.

The bombing of the reactor prevented an unfathomable disaster.

Operation "Desert Storm" and the liberation of Kuwait, were possible only thanks to Israel bombing of the nuclear reactor in Iraq. Otherwise, it is likely that world reaction would have been hesitant if at all.

Um-Shmum we said already.

Maybe I am deviating a bit from the subject, but out of intellectual curiosity I assembled data about the global nuclear arsenal [29] and the extent of destruction it can create. With your permission I will present it here briefly:

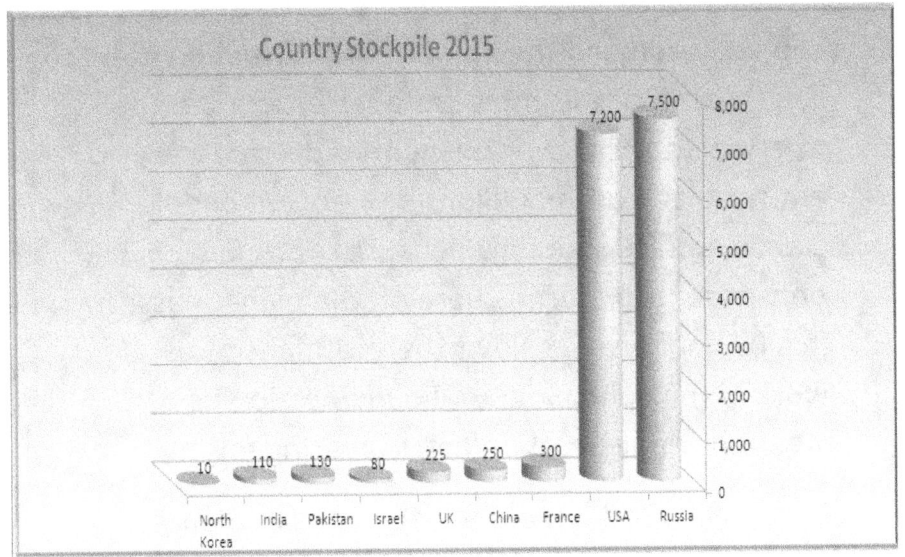

* From a report published on July 23rd 2015
http://ploughshares.org/world-nuclear-stockpile-report

(29) http://www.ploughshares.org/news-analysis/world-nuclear-stockpile-report

The amount of nuclear weapons is huge, with over 15,000 warheads.

In World War II, "small" nuclear bombs were sufficient to lead to the surrender of Japan following the destruction of 2 major cities in Japan: "Nagasaki" and "Hiroshima". Can anyone imagine what energy 20,000 nuclear warheads have?

And let us not forget that since "Nagasaki" and "Hiroshima, nuclear weapons have become more sophisticated and the amount of destruction they can cause today is immeasurably enormous. The existing weapons are sufficient to destroy the entire solar system. Billions of innocent people can evaporate suddenly because of some nonsense. Our journey here on the planet passes in a blink of an eye. Nevertheless, many of us work in the course of our life on developing weapons of destruction or on creating misery.

This is our big missed opportunity as human beings. We failed to use our brain to create affluence but created misery. We are used to think that affluence must come at the expense of the other, and in the universe there is not enough affluence for everybody.

Thus too few members in the human club have a home, relish in endless gluttony, leave food on the plate and a significant part of the residents of the western part of the planet turn into walking potatoes, while millions of people in Africa and in developing countries around the world live on a pinch of food.

One side doesn't know satiety, and the other side does not know hunger.

Doesn`t this seem a bit unreal, that in a certain part of the world people spend enormous amounts of money to learn how not to eat, and in the other part of the world people have no money to buy food.

MAKES NO SENSE!

"Little Boy" is the code name of the atomic bomb that was dropped on Hiroshima on August 6th, 1945. It is estimated that the energy of the explosion was approximately 13 to 16 kiloton TNT. The destruction of Hiroshima by the bomb caused approximately 140,000 deaths.

As the megabytes in the high-tech world replaced the kilobytes, and later on the gigabytes replaced the megabytes, and in the next stage the terabytes will probably replace the gigabytes, thus also the evolution of nuclear bombs progressed. When talking today about nuclear bombs we talk about mega, and just like in computers, each megaton contains 1,000 kilotons.

During the Cold War, the United States and the Soviet Union have been working on developing and increasing the nuclear arsenal. The Soviet Union broke the record when it conducted a nuclear experiment with a bomb that was nicknamed "The Czar`s Bomb". This was the biggest and the strongest bomb (hydrogen) ever tested. The energy of the explosion that was created following the bombing was about 50 mega tons. The energy of the explosion created by the bomb was about 50 mega tons, about 3,500 times the energy "The Little Boy" that was dropped on Hiroshima during World War II. Can you imagine that? A bomb with an energy equivalent to 3,500 atomic bombs that were dropped on Hiroshima.

MAKES NO SENSE!

The State of Israel is blessed with a miniature area and with narrow borders that are surrounded by uncompromising enemies. The distances are ridiculously short. Israel cannot afford a nuclear threat, and one bomb could wipe her off the map.

Israel should not expect the "free world" to help it in time of need.

The technology of that "free world" is helping to build today the nuclear reactors in Iran. I am sitting now in my lovely apartment in mid-January. It is winter outside with very heavy rains. The heater is on and the truth is that it is quite pleasant. The girls have already gone to sleep and I am free to write. I inhabit in the center of the country yet half an hour of jogging and I am by the sea. On the other hand, the distance between me and the hostile border, is no more than 20 kilometers.

As a Jew in the State of Israel I have learned to accept things not for granted.

THE UNITED NATIONS AS AN OBSTACLE

Quite often the UN stations its soldiers in conflict zones in order to prevent the recurrence of hostilities. Such a force was stationed also on the Israel-Lebanon border. This force was watching the Hezbollah [(30)] on Saturday October 7th 2000 towards lunch-time when the Hezbollah entered Israel in order to attack Israel Defense Force soldiers and to abduct 3 soldiers.

The Hezbollah attacked an unfortified patrol vehicle of the IDF that was patrolling along the border fence in the Mount Dov region, near the Shebaa village. The UN soldiers knew about the preparations in progress, documented them in video and concealed the tape from the world. The existence of the tape leaked, but UN officials denied that there was any such tape. Almost a year later, in June 2001, it was revealed that the UN headquarters in New York posses photos of the abduction. The video was filmed by UNIFIL soldiers [(31)] (the Indian battalion) who were stationed in an outpost overlooking the abduction area, and it contained also a scan made at the point of abduction on the Lebanese side.

The UN people took also photos of Hezbollah men transferring the abducted soldiers about 18 hours after the incident, about 19 kilometers only away from where they were kidnapped. The event was documented, and the UN tried unsuccessfully to cover it up. [32]

---

[30] The Hezbollah is a terror organization that was founded as a militia in 1982 (officially in 1985), with funding and equipment by Iran, its patron. The Hezbollah, being a Shiite fundamentalist organization, aims to convert Lebanon to be the same. The organization considers the State of Israel as its main enemy and acts against it with all the means at its disposal. As far as the organization is concerned, the area governed by Israel is "occupied Palestine" taken over by the "Zionist enemy". From Wikipedia under the entry: "Hezbollah".

[31] United Nations Interim Force in Lebanon.

[32] Source: Wikipedia, under the entry: "The abduction of the soldiers at Mount Dov".

Thus, the UN that was supposed to prevent the abduction not only did not prevent it but rather assisted in its success. Instead of doing its job and warn the State of Israel about the preparations for the abduction and the violation of a series of international laws, it made sure to document the abduction and conceal it.

Um - Shmum.

What was it that bothered Ben Ki-Moon, the UN Secretary General, on 03/11/2009?

Was it a few more thousands of deaths in Darfur? No!

Was it riots in Iran during which dissidents were put away by the authorities? No!

Was it the global hunger problems? No!

Maybe the global warming? This is rubbish!

Maybe the North Korean nuclear threat? No, this doesn`t disturb even a siesta.

And maybe, the threat of Iran developing a nuclear bomb? Don`t talk nonsense.

The Secretary-General was horrified by Israel's actions. Jews entered a house in East Jerusalem with the Court`s approval.[33]

A building that belonged to Jews even before the establishment of the State, and the question of ownership of the building has been in litigation for decades.

A minor problem, no? Someone invaded the house you purchased with your own money and after years of legal struggle, the court upheld you take possession of the house.

What has the Secretary-General Ban Ki-moon to do with the evacuation of an invading family? What about it causes him such anxiety?

When terror attacks against Jews happen in Israel, he does not say a word. When rockets are fired almost every day at Israeli cities, he does not say a word.

---

(33)
http://www.unmultimedia.org/radio/english/detail/85059.html

Four months later, in the first week of March 2010, a few disturbing things happened. Every week a few disturbing things happen in the world.

Nevertheless, today there are about 425 conflicts around the world.

What happened in the world this week?

1. In Nigeria, about 500 Christians were slaughtered within 3 hours by a Muslim mob. [34] The massacre began in the middle of the night, when Muslims invaded the Christian villages and drove the residents out of their homes by shootings in the air. When they were out, the Muslims began to slaughter them with swords and machetes. Those who remained in the houses were burned alive when their huts were set on fire.

The survivors bury their loved ones (AFP PHOTO /PIUS UTOMI EKPEI)

The Minister of Information in the State of Plateau, Gregory Janlong, updated that over 500 people lost their lives in the brutal massacre. The survivors buried their loved ones. He emphasized that many of those slaughtered were children and pregnant women who were attacked with axes, daggers and shovels.

---

(34) http://allafrica.com/stories/201003090510.html

Corrine Dobka, senior researcher of West Africa in the Human Right Watch Organization, said that this horrible violence has claimed the lives of thousands of victims in the State of Plateau itself in the last decade, however no one was prosecuted. (35)

2. The UN notable, Iran's former President, spoke again in the port city Bandar-Abbas a

speech that was broadcasted in the local television stations. According to him, the western world gathered the most criminal people in the world in Israel. "Israel launched wars and acts of aggression that have made millions of people homeless". After the hate speech, came the grand finale in which he claimed that the Zionist regime is the most hated regime in the world. "It has lost the support of the West and therefore whether Israel wants it or not this regime, Allah willing, will be wiped out." [36]

Israel is a barrier between Iran and the rest of the non-Muslim world. The President of Iran has already stated in the past that the struggle is between Islam and Christianity. In the past 300 years Islam has lost, but according to the vision of the President of Iran, this is going to change. People of the Earth: if you continue to wear your pink glasses you will find yourselves before long removing them in favor of veils. Maybe a short reminder will help you:

From the speech by Ahmadinejad: "A war with ancient roots has been going on between the arrogant and conceited world and the Muslim world. In this historic war the battlefields have changed many times. Sometimes the Muslims had the upper hand and sometimes it was the other way round. Unfortunately, in the last three hundred years the Muslim world has retreated from the arrogant ones.

---

(35) More about that can be found in an article published in the Ynet website under the title: "Nigeria is asking: what caused the shocking massacre?" (Published on 09.03.10)

(36) From an article published in the Ynet website under the title: "Ahmadinejad: Israel that is hated around the world - and it will be destroyed" (published on 11.03.10)

About a hundred years ago the last bastion of Islam fell, when the repressive authorities established the Zionist regime. This regime serves as a front stronghold in the heart of the Muslim world. The struggle over the occupied land is part of a war on the destiny. The outcome of hundreds of years of war will be determined in Palestine. There are those who wonder if the day will come when we will see a world without the United States and the Zionists. This goal is indeed realizable. There is no doubt that we are at the outset of a wave in Palestine that will wash the disgraceful blemish (Israel) off the face of the Muslim world".[37]

Does it interest anyone that the President of a Member State of the UN wishes to destroy another Member State of the UN?

Probably not.

PHOTO/Martyn Wheatley

(37) Translation of the speech from the website -
http://www.globalsecurity.org/military/world/iran/zionist-entity-2.htm

3. Israel's Ministry of Interior approved the construction of 1,600 residential units in the eastern part of Israel's capital, Jerusalem. A few hours after the approval, the Secretary-General of the UN was shocked to such an extent, that he issued an angry statement in which he condemned the approval. Not a word about the President of Iran or the massacre in Nigeria, after all the Nigerians are not really human beings, and the former President of Iran just took off some steam (the Israelis are again trampling on the international law and are committing shocking acts that violate the stability of the world).

An article, published in The Jerusalem Post, [38] describes the lack of symmetry in the news coverage that the Israeli-Palestinian conflict gets and the amount of condemnations that Israel gets compared to the "genocide" that is committed in Sudan.

I selected a few interesting paragraphs from the article: [39]

"The behavior of the UN with regard to Israel is distorted and hypocritical. The Human Rights

Council of the UN convened for the first time regarding the massacre in Darfur in December 2006. The Council did not bother at the end of the conference to condemn the Sudanese government for the shocking massacre in which over 450,000 people were slaughtered. At the same time the Council adopted not less than 3 resolutions condemning Israel. The Secretary-General of the UN at the time, Kofi Annan, referred to the condemnations as disproportionate.

"In the same way, the UN General Assembly devotes 3 full days in November of each year, to discuss and condemn Israeli "occupation". If you fail to remember any recurring sessions regarding Darfur, the problem is not your memory. In summary, the UN General Assembly has received no fewer than 25 resolutions condemning the violations of Human Rights committed by Israel, but did not see fit to condemn even once the horrible massacre in Darfur."

---

(38) An Israeli daily newspaper in English.

(39) Evelyn Gordon "Lost in the Palestinians' shadow", THE JERUSALEM POST, Jan. 3, 2007.

Apparently Congo, Iraq, Afghanistan, Darfur, North Korea, Taiwan, Chad, Syria, Libya etc. are not urgent issues. In contrast, the "Palestinian" problem is so urgent and important for global agenda that they were granted not less than 6 subsidiary bodies under the General Assembly while no organization that is a Member of the UN has been allocated dedicated bodies.

"The UN has many bodies, such as the Standing Committee on the rights of the "Palestinian people" that is dedicated exclusively to the Israeli-Palestinian conflict. The Palestinian refugees have an agency of their own, UNRWA (United Nation Relief and Works Agency) while the rest of the refugees in the world are "competing" for the attention of the UN High Commissioner for Refugees. Hence, is it surprising that 3,000,000 Darfur refugees are lost in the shadow of the Palestinians?"[40]

In November 29th 1947 the UN General Assembly voted for the establishment of a State for the Jewish people. This symbolic significance has been grounded and trampled by the Palestinians, who chose this date as the International Day of Solidarity with the Palestinian people.

The UN adopted this date warmly. Traditionally the UN makes anti-Israeli resolutions on this date. In this way the Muslim propaganda manufactures de-legitimization of Israel.

So next time the UN condemns the State of Israel for the war crimes that it commits, ask yourself what the UN did on that day to prevent the ongoing genocide in the Darfur region! What did the UN do to prevent the ongoing brutal murder by ISIS in the areas under its control.

---

(40) "Lost in the Palestinians' shadow", Jan. 3, 2007 , Evelyn Gordon , THE JERUSALEM POST

The number of Member States in the UN is 204. If you are holding this book in your hands, it is most likely that you live in a democracy. If this book is not handy or it did not receive marketing approval, it is likely that you live in a dictatorship. Does anybody know what is the percentage of democratic Member States in the UN?

The answer is: 46%.

MAKES NO SENSE!

That is to say, that even today, more than 50% of
the countries in the world are not democracies.
Namely, Human Rights are not a built-in principle
in society, and most citizens are at the mercy of
the regime, or at the whims of an absolute
monarch.

To summarize the activities of the UN to prevent
atrocities, a table of only the major events is
presented herewith:

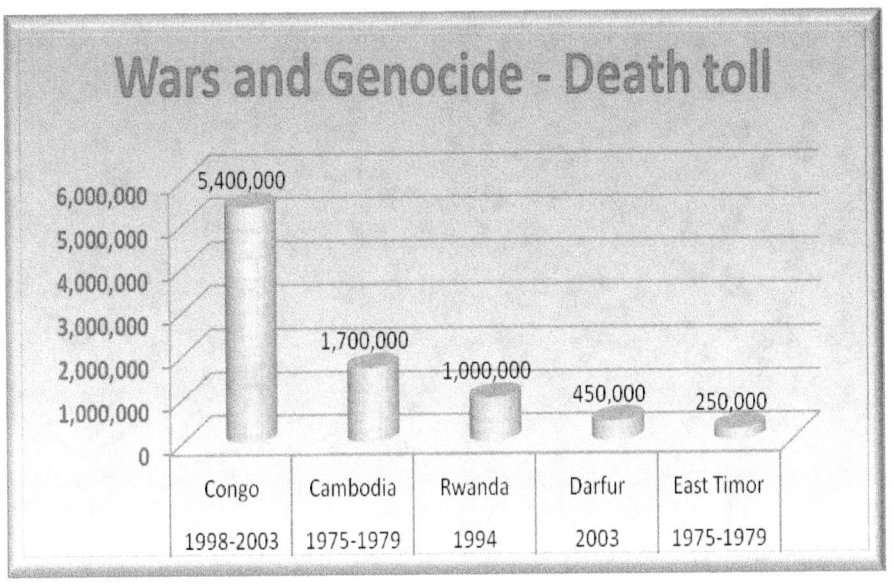

The continued table will include, among others, Syria, Iraq, Libya, Yemen, where civil wars have been going on since 2011 with the outbreak of the "Arab Spring" revolution.

"NEVER AGAIN!", YEAH – SURE.

EPILOGUE

To conclude the chapter: this book was written during a turbulent period in the Middle East. From time to time, when I thought that I have exhausted everything I had to write on a certain subject and I moved on to the next one, events occurred that made me go back to previous chapters and update them.

There is no end to it, of course, and during this period the Middle East is changing before our eyes. While daydreamers throughout the Western world are fantasizing about democracies popping up like mushrooms after the rain, in the Middle East a bloody war is going on in regions that were once called Syria and Iraq and there is, of course, leakage to Yemen and Libya. The death toll has crossed the hundreds of thousands.

Let's examine again what happened on one specific day. Well, in May 2010, 9 "peace activists" armed with clubs, axes, knives and chains were killed while they were on the ship "Marmara" that was sailing to the Gaza Strip in order to help "their besieged brethren". The Security Council convened quickly and condemned Israel.

I am still waiting to see that same Council convene and condemn Syria for the massacre of its own residents that it commits.

Is it not strange that Syria endorses the resolution that condemns Israel and accuses it for violating human rights?

MAKES NO SENSE!

A separate and unique Article, called Article 7, is reserved for the condemnation of Israel.

For all the other countries in the world, including Yemen, Syria and Libya, Article 4 is dedicated, an Article that describes human rights around the world.

There are violations of human rights which are okay. Such as, for instance,   slaughters in Sudan, Congo, Libya, Yemen, Syria, Iraq and more. And there are violations of human rights that are wrong. These - are committed only in Israel!

To deepen the understsanding of the Middle East I welcome you to read the series of books I wrote on this matter.

You can find them under my name Kobi Shashoua On Amazon or on the website:
www.kobisha.com

Please feel free to contact me via email:
kobimnsil@gmail.com

Tel: 972-54-8030648

Sincerely,

Kobi Shashoua